Spot the Difference

Seeds

Charlotte Guillain

www.heinemann.co.uk/library
Visit our website to find out more information about Heinemann Library books.

To order:
☎ Phone 44 (0) 1865 888066
📄 Send a fax to 44 (0) 1865 314091
🖥 Visit the Heinemann Bookshop at www.heinemann.co.uk/library to browse our catalogue and order online.

First published in Great Britain by Heinemann Library, Halley Court, Jordan Hill, Oxford OX2 8EJ, part of Harcourt Education. Heinemann is a registered trademark of Harcourt Education Ltd.

Editorial: Sian Smith and Cassie Mayer
Design: Joanna Hinton-Malivoire
Picture research: Erica Martin and Hannah Taylor
Production: Duncan Gilbert

Printed and bound in China by South China Printing Co. Ltd

ISBN 978 0 431 19232 1

12 11 10 09 08
10 9 8 7 6 5 4 3 2 1

British Library Cataloguing in Publication Data
Guillain, Charlotte
  Seeds. - (Spot the difference)
  1. Seeds - Juvenile literature
  I. Title
  581.4'67

Acknowledgements
The publishers would like to thank the following for permission to reproduce photographs: ©Alamy pp.**18**, **23a** (Christopher Griffin); ©Bjanka Kadic pp.**12**, **23c** (flowerphotos.com); ©Corbis pp.**5** (PBNJ Productions/PBNJ Productions), **10 right** (louds Hill Imaging Ltd); ©FLPA pp.**7**, **23b** (Inga Spence), **19** (John Watkins), **6** (Nigel Cattlin); ©Geoscience Features Picture Library p.**16** (Dr.B.Booth); ©Getty Images p.**15** (Science Faction); ©istockphoto.com pp.**4 bottom right** (Stan Rohrer), **4 top left** (CHEN PING-HUNG), **4 top right** (John Pitcher), **10 left** (ranplett), **4 bottom left** (Vladimir Ivanov); ©Nature picture library pp. **13**, **23d** (Jose B. Ruiz); ©Photolibrary pp.**11**, **22 left** (Botanica), **8**, **9**, **21**, (Animals Animals / Earth Scenes), **14**, **22 right** (Mark Bolton), **17** (Satoshi Kuribayashi); ©Science photo library p**20** (Larry Miller).

Cover photograph of coral bean seeds reproduced with permission of ©Photolibrary (Animals Animals / Earth Scenes). Back cover photograph of horse chestnut seeds reproduced with permission of ©Bjanka Kadic (flowerphotos.com).

Every effort has been made to contact copyright holders of any material reproduced in this book. Any omissions will be rectified in subsequent printings if notice is given to the publishers.

Contents

What are plants?

Plants are living things.
Plants live in many places.

Plants need air to grow.
Plants need water to grow.
Plants need sunlight to grow.

What are seeds?

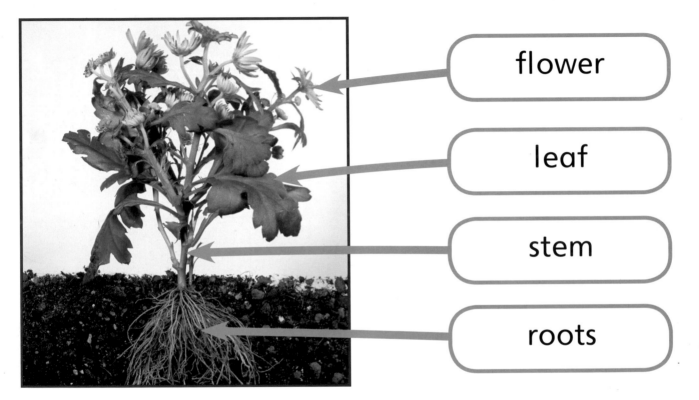

flower

leaf

stem

roots

Plants have many parts.
A seed is a part of a plant.

Plants grow from seeds.

Different seeds

These are sunflower seeds.
They are black.

These are coral bean seeds.
They are red.

seed

This is a strawberry.
It has very small seeds.

seed

This is a coconut tree.
It has very big seeds.

These are horse chestnut seeds.
They are smooth.

These are cranesbill seeds.
They are spiky.

Amazing seeds

These are sycamore seeds.
They have wings to carry them.

These are dandelion seeds.
They have hairs to carry them.

This is a goosegrass seed.
It has hooks so animals can carry it.

This is a trillium seed.
It is small so insects can carry it.

These are beech seeds.
They float in water.

These are mistletoe seeds.
They stick to birds.

What do seeds do?

Seeds travel to a new place.

seed

Seeds grow into
new plants.

Spot the difference!

How many differences can you see?

Picture glossary

 **float** to stay on top of water

 **seed** grows into a new plant. Plants make seeds.

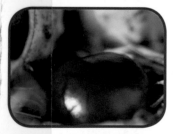 **smooth** flat; does not have bumps

 **spiky** has sharp points

Index

Notes to parents and teachers

Before reading

Show the children seeds of different colours e.g. some mixed bird seed. Talk to the children about how most plants grow from seeds. Even the very big trees start from a seed. Explain that the seeds come from the flower of a plant. When they drop to the ground, they begin to grow and make a new plant.

After reading

• Give each child a polystyrene tray. Place damp newspaper in the tray. Using grass seed, sprinkle the outline of the initial letter of the child's name. Watch the letter grow!

• Show the children some seeds we eat e.g. peas, beans, cucumbers, strawberries, and corn. Show them seeds that we do not eat, from other fruit e.g. apples, melons, oranges, or peaches.

• To the tune of 'The Farmer's in his Den' sing the following song: The farmer plants his seed (2). Deep down in the ground the farmer plants his seed. Make up other verses e.g. The rain falls on the seed. The sun gives warmth and light etc.